Contents

Puns Galore

First Mexican woman: Your boyfriend is very handsome.
Second Mexican woman: If you think he's handsome, you should have seen the Juan that got away.

A man asked a priest, "Father, do you remember me?"
The priest answered, "I don't remember your name, but your faith is familiar."

The man who constantly complained always went to bed early and got up at the *crank* of dawn.

1

A man who sometimes seemed depressed, then at other times seemed happy, said "What I believe is, easy glum, easy glow."

What did the Indian chief call his wife?
Sweet Sioux.

The man who kept borrowing money was feeling very LOANLY.

Dead vocalists have the STIFF that singers are made of.

A computer date is a *calculated* risk.

Dad has a magnetic personality—every time he buys something, he *charges*.

When mom asked dad to start a garden, the first thing he dug up was an excuse.

Books are made from paper which comes from trees.
Is that why we have BRANCH libraries?

When the famous artist Whistler saw his mother standing by the window he shouted, "Good heavens mother—have you gone off your rocker?"

Is a pirate ship a *thug* boat?

3

Why does winter seem so long?

Because it comes in one year and out the other.

When does a baby awake?

In the wee-wee hours of the morning.

One angry Italian woman told her husband, "I'm gonna give you a pizza my mind!"

"It's raining cats and dogs."

"I know—I just stepped in a poodle."

"Remember—when you leave the room, switch off the lights."

"Thanks a watt!"

A bachelor is a man who is foot loose and *fiancée* free.

Prices on most goods are continually going up, but the price of writing paper has remained STATIONERY.

Coal is one substance that first goes to the buyer, then goes directly to the CELLAR.

Slot machines are contraptions that are COINivorous.

A sign in a bar read:
   THIRST COME, THIRST SERVED.

At a masquerade party it's easy to tell the good GUISE from the bad.

What we've been hearing about spray cans is enough to SCAREOSOL to death.

Mom: Why are you standing on your head?
Daughter: I'm trying to turn things over in my mind.

The little boy told his father, "When I grow up I want to drive a giant army tank."

"Well," said his father, "if that's what you really want, I certainly won't stand in your way!"

Why did the little boy throw his clock out of the window?
    He wanted to see time fly.

Why did the inventor design a better lawn mower?
    He wanted to make mower money.

Many tired people like to sit down for a spell and have a quiet game of Scrabble.

What happened to the inventor of lighter fluid?
  He became flamous.

Eskimos can see very well—they have good ICE sight.

What did the Leaning Tower of Pisa say to Big Ben?
  "If you've got the time, I've got the inclination."

England has a blood bank; it also has a Liverpool.

Did you hear about the lunatic who climbed the Eiffel Tower, then jumped into the river? You might say he went in Seine (insane).

A group of American tourists flew to Santiago. When they arrived they got a Chile reception.

First Hunter: How are you enjoying the visit to Africa?
Second Hunter: Safari, so good.

Why can you never starve at a beach?
  Because of the sand which (sandwich) is there.

Wife: How did you catch the Persian plane?
Husband: Iran.

The husband wanted to visit the Middle East while his wife wanted to see South America. He told her, "You go Uruguay, I'll go mine."

8

My sister came home from the beach as red as a ripe tomato—she got more sun than she basked for!

The barber shop got very hot in the summer, so the owner had it HAIR-conditioned.

Is the guillotine a French *chopping* center?

Did you hear about the two lenses that got together and made a *spectacle* of themselves?

What is racial superiority?
  It's a pigment of the imagination.

When's a door not a door?
    When it's ajar.

This spy novel is so gripping that I had to read it from covert to covert.

He called me woodenhead, so I gave him a piece of my mind.

The electric chair is a good example of period furniture— after all, it ends a sentence.

Who invented the first pen?
    The Incas (inkers).

What's the difference between Noah's Ark and Joan of Arc?
One was made of wood—the other was Maid of Orleans.

Name the world's most shocking city.
ElectriCITY.

Daughter: Dirty plastic spoons, garbage, broken bottles, dented cans . . .
Father: Would you stop talking trash!

Andrea: Where does your mother come from?
Susan: Alaska.
Andrea: Don't bother—I'll ask her myself.

What did the acorn say when it grew up?
  Geometry! (Gee I'm a tree)

What's bought by the yard and worn by the feet?
  A carpet.

Adam and Eve decided to open a business. They hung a sign in the window which read: WE'RE NEVER CLOTHED.

Who invented the first fireplace?
  Alexander the Grate.

Boy magnet to girl magnet—"I find you so attractive."

Sign seen in a florist's window:
    WE ARE A GROWING BUSINESS.

"That was a good yolk," he CRACKED.

"The furnace is giving us trouble," he FUMED.

"Don't needle me," he said POINTEDLY.

"We've struck oil," he GUSHED.

"I love onions," she CRIED.

13

"Turn off the fridge," he said ICILY.

"Turn down the thermostat," she said HEATEDLY.

"Drop the gun," he said DISARMINGLY.
"Never," he SHOT back.

Did you hear about the man was was driving very fast?
He approached the coroner at 80 miles an hour.

Sign in a tire shop: WE SKID YOU NOT.

Man: How's your son coming along with his driving lessons?

Friend: Last week he took a turn for the worse.

Road sign: DRIVE RIGHT SO MORE PEOPLE WILL BE LEFT.

A stupid motorist saw this sign: FINE FOR PARKING. So he parked!

A wife insisted her husband buy her a Jaguar for Christmas.

So he did, and the very next day it ate her up.

15

The Spaniards were experts at fuel conservation. They could go for thousands of miles on a GALLEON.

Man: Which of these cars will provide the best mileage?
Salesman: Your gas is as good as mine.

A good many family squabbles over the new car start from scratch.

They don't make cars like they auto.

What did the grape say when an ape stepped on it?
   Nothing—it just gave a little whine!

What close relatives do boy robots have?
   Tran-SISTERS.

One robot had a nervous breakdown. The doctor diagnosed it as METAL fatigue.

When Einstein told a joke, it really was a WISEcrack.

Did you hear about the guy who stayed up all night trying to figure out where the sun disappeared when it went down?
   It finally dawned on him.

What did one atom say to another atom?
   "Let's split."

A scientist who's studying mummies is in danger of becoming wrapped up in his work.

Girl: What's an archaeologist?
Mom: A man whose career lies in ruins.

Astronaut—a whirled traveler.

It's said that Isaac Newton discovered gravity when an apple hit him on the head. If that's true, the discovery must have shaken him to the *core*!

If athletes suffer from athlete's foot, what do astronauts suffer from?
    Mistletoe.

Some people think the North Pole and the South Pole are similar.

It's not true—there's all the difference in the world between them.

Astronauts are highly successful people—after all, they always go up in the world.

An astronaut's career is short-lived—soon after they're hired, they're fired!

What would happen if you swallowed uranium?
  You'd get atomic ache.

Where do astronauts leave their spaceships?
   At parking meteors.

Why is the space program so expensive?
   Because there's no limit to the overheads.

The inventor of the safety match was a STRIKING success.

The clock was a TIMELY invention.

Teacher: How did Benjamin Franklin first find out about electricity?
Student: It came to him in a flash!

What did Ben Franklin say when he realized the importance of his discovery?
Nothing—he was too shocked!

Why did the germ walk across the microscope?
To get to the other slide.

Why did Mickey Mouse take a trip to outer space?
He wanted to find Pluto.

Why don't astronauts get hungry after being blasted into outer space?

Because they've just had a big LAUNCH.

What did the astronaut see in the pan?

An unidentified frying object.

Two astronauts were asked, "How do you like your work?"

One replied, "It's heavenly."

The other said, "It has its ups and downs!"

What breed of dog would you expect a chemistry professor to have?

A laboratory retriever.

Astronauts are thought to be STAR-CRAVING mad.

An astronomer was asked, "How's business?"
   He answered, "It's looking up."

What did the astronomer say when asked to describe the heavenly body with a long tail that travels through space?
   "No comet!"

How do you get a baby astronaut to sleep?
   Rock-et.

An atomic scientist hung a sign on his office door when he went on vacation which read: "GONE FISSION."

When soda was first bottled, the inventor's son said, "That's my POP!"

What did the Martian say when he landed?
"We're here by accident—we didn't planet this way."

What might astronauts wear to keep themselves warm?
Apollo shirts.

One thing you can say about Isaac Newton—he was a down-to-earth man.

What famous insect comes from outer space?
BUG Rogers.

Flying saucer—a dish that's out of this world!

Why are robots never afraid?
  Because they have nerves of steel.

A crazy scientist put dynamite in his fridge. I guess you might say he blew his cool.

What do you call a crazy spaceman?
  An astronut.

What's the favorite meal of nuclear scientists?
  Fission chips.

Men who fly to the moon are LUNAtics!

How do you tell the sex of a chromosome?
  Pull down its genes.

Manuel Workers and Seville Servants

What did the hotel owner advertise for?
 Someone who was INN-experienced.

What does an electrician like to read about?
 CURRENT events.

Did you hear about the sculptor who complained he was always being taken for granite?

A shoemaker opened a small shop—he was the *sole* proprietor.

The car mechanic complained, "Installing mufflers is *exhausting* work."

Manufacturers of percussion instruments are not doing so well. They have to go out and drum up business!

"How do you like your job?" they asked the baker.
"I'm in loaf with it," he answered.

Do you know what happened to the man who invented the relief map?

He got a raise!

How do you know the carpenter was nervous?

He always bit his nails.

How is the dynamite manufacturer doing?

His business is BOOMING!

Why are candlemakers on strike?

They're demanding longer wick ends (weekends).

A man worked as a personal driver for a millionaire. After twenty years of service, he had nothing to *chauffeur* it.

How do you become a coroner?
  You have to take a STIFF examination.

It's claimed that fishermen are never generous.
  It's because of their business—it makes them sell fish (selfish).

Why was the man in the car factory fired?
  He was caught taking a brake!

What do you call Spanish laborers?
  Manuel workers.

Termites are boring—they work with all termite.

What did the wig-maker ask the customer?
  "How do you want toupee the bill?"

How do you become an executioner?
  Just axe!

Why was the nurse fired?
  She kept needling all her patients.

What type of people apart from doctors are employed in a
hospital?
  Those who can do things in an *orderly* fashion.

31

Working on a rig in the North Sea means oily to bed and oily to rise.

What does a doctor need to be successful?
   Plenty of patience (patients).

What happened to the glass-blower when he inhaled?
   He got a pane in his stomach.

A fish-processing factory had so many orders that the manager said they couldn't fillet!

Did you hear about the librarian who always looked sad because her books were in tiers?

Outside a cemetery was a notice which read:

"Owing to the strike by grave-diggers, graves will be dug by a SKELETON staff."

How do we know that Robinson Crusoe was a fast worker?
Because he always had all his work done by Friday.

I've just heard the news—apparently watchmakers are going on strike for more overtime.

The clockmaker said, "Every morning I rise and chime!"

"How do you like your job as an elevator operator?"
"It has its ups and downs."

What's another word for soda jerk?
  A fizzician.

I know of one cabinet maker who refers to himself as a counter fitter.

What's a magician?
  A super duper.

What kind of person was the man who built ships?
  One hull-uva guy!

Writers have to be careful—they can easily get authoritis.

Did you hear about the boss who hired two of his sons to work in his office? He was accused of putting on heirs.

34

I can't understand why the dressmaker closed her shop—she SEAMED to be doing very well.

I know a man who got fired because of illness and fatigue. The boss got sick and tired of him!

There's a man at Pennsylvania Station who shines shoes—he calls himself a BOOTician.

Did the fortune-teller enjoy her work?
Yes indeed—she always had a ball!

An X-ray technician is one person who always gets the real *inside* story.

Why did the bakers go on strike?
   They wanted more dough.

Who is always being let down by his mates?
   A deep-sea diver.

The new switchboard operator was having difficulty learning her job, but she kept *plugging* away at it.

When the tailor was asked how he liked his job, he answered, "Sew-sew."

How do we know that the clock manufacturer is crazy?
   Because he only makes cuckoo clocks.

What's a shoe seller's favorite tune?
  "There's no business like shoe business . . . "

Who gets the sack every time he goes to work?
  The postman.

Why was the well-dressed man chosen for the job?
  He was obviously the best-suited for the position.

The man who fixed Big Ben thought of himself as a big-time operator.

What are government workers called in Spain?
  Seville servants.

A plumber is forever having pipe dreams.

Old burglars never die—they just *steal* away.

What did the president of the tailors' union ask for from the newspapers?
   A PRESS conference.

Vegetable farmers from all over the world intend to have an international meeting. It will be the first PEAS conference.

What was given to the graduates of the diving school?
   DEEP-lomas (diplomas).

Just for the Halibut

What fish might you find in a bird cage?
  A perch.

Which fish feels the most comfortable on ice?
  A skate.

What do you call a whale that talks too much?
  A blubber mouth.

Where do you go to weigh a whale?
  To the whaleweigh station.

What's the best fish to eat with peanut butter?
  Jellyfish.

What do police fish ride in?
  A squid car.

Name the sea creature used for transportation.
  An octobus.

Why didn't the sharks eat the woman who fell overboard?
  Because they were man-eaters.

How did Jonah feel when he was swallowed by a whale?
  Down in the mouth.

Why did the fish cross the road?
  To get to the other tide.

What do you get if you cross a whale with a bird?
  Moby Duck.

Why are fish smart?
  Because they travel in schools.

What's biased, hates other fish, wears white sheets, and lives at the bottom of the ocean?
  Ku Klux Clam.

41

The life of a fish is ova before it begins.

What makes an eel happy?
  Being head over eels in love.

Why are fishermen wealthy?
  Because their business is net profit.

What did one fisherman say to his friend when they met in the middle of the desert?
  "Hi—long time no sea."

What do you call a nutty octopus?
  A crazy mixed-up squid.

How do you communicate with a fish?
  Drop him a line.

What do you call a young whale?
  A small squirt.

How do you catch an electric eel?
  With a lightning rod.

Why couldn't Batman go fishing?
  'Cause Robin ate all the worms.

Why are lobsters so often arrested?
  Because they're always pinching things.

When fish go into business, they usually start on a small scale.

Did you hear about the sardine who kept getting to work late?
One day he got canned!

What fish will make you an offer you can't refuse?
The Codfather.

What fish leaves yellow footprints on the ocean floor?
A lemon sole.

What whizzes through the water at a hundred miles an hour?
A motor-pike.

How do you keep a fish from smelling?
   Cut off its nose.

Where can you see a man-eating fish?
   In a seafood restaurant.

What part of the fish weighs the most?
   The scales.

Which fish travels the greatest distance?
   Goldfish—they travel around the globe.

"*Do you like codfish balls?*"
   "I don't know—I've never been to one."

A fish was having trouble with its ears—it was becoming hard of HERRING.

A shark was playing an out-of-tune piano. Who should it call?
A piano tuna.

Who can operate on a sick fish?
A sturgeon.

One fish caught the measles. But it wasn't so bad—he only had them on a small scale.

A conference of important fish in the sea was postponed so the fish could first MULLET over.

When a fish wants a face lift, it goes to a plastic sturgeon.

There's a new fish hook on the market—it's really caught on!

Why do fishermen fish?
  Just for the halibut.

What do young fish like to play?
  Carps and robbers.

Did you hear about the driver who tied a shark to the front and back of his car? He thinks of them as *shark absorbers*.

Fish: How do you like the water in this part of the ocean?
Sponge: Absorbing!

Cross an owl with a skunk and you'll wind up with a bird that smells horrible, but doesn't give a hoot.

What did the owner give his pet canary when it was one year old?
   A birday party.

Why did the farmer hire birds to harvest his crop?
   Because they were cheep labor.

What bird can lift the most weight?
   The crane.

What kind of film do geese like to watch?
    Duck-umentaries.

Which bird can be heard at every meal?
    The swallow.

Where are water birds taken when they feel sick?
    To the duck-tor.

Jungle commandment—HONOR THY PARROTS.

"If you want your parrot to talk you should begin by teaching it short words."

"Really? I thought it would be quicker to use POLLY-syllables."

What kind of hens lay electric eggs?
  Battery hens.

Cross a chicken with a cement mixer and you wind up with a brick layer.

How is a goose like a car?
  They both go honk!

What kind of berries do geese eat?
  Goose-berries.

A crow is a bird that never complains without CAWS.

What do you call a crazy crow?
  A raven maniac.

What did the blackbird say to the scarecrow?
  "I can knock the stuffin' out of you."

Birds never have to worry about money—two can always live as CHEEPLY as one.

What's used to stuff a dead parrot?
  Pollyfilla.

Why did the sparrow fly into the library?
  It was looking for bookworms.

Why shouldn't you tell secrets to a peacock?
   Because they're known to spread tails (tales).

What do you get when you cross a bird and a zero?
   A flying none (nun).

Which bird is always out of breath?
   The puffin.

Mother pigeon: Either you learn to fly, or I'll tie a string around your leg and tow you.
Baby pigeon: Oh, Mommy—I'd rather die than be pigeon-toed.

What kind of birds do we usually find in captivity?
   Jailbirds.

What's green and pecks at trees?
  Woody Woodpickle.

Why don't people like to hear stories about woodpeckers?
  Because they're boring.

What do you call a very intelligent owl?
  A birdbrain.

Cross an owl with an oyster and you'll wind up with a bird that drops pearls of wisdom.

What do you call a shop that sells pets which can swim and fly?
  A fish and cheep shop.

What happened after the chicken drank some whisky?
  It laid Scotch eggs.

Where do birds invest their money?
  In the stork market.

Which birds are always unhappy?
  Bluebirds.

Name the rudest of all birds.
  The mockingbird.

What bird can be found in a coal pit?
  A Myna bird.

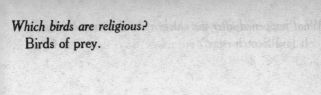

Which birds are religious?
   Birds of prey.

My teacher does bird imitations—she watches me like a hawk!

If a chicken crosses the road, rolls in the mud and crosses back again, what do you have?
   A dirty double-crosser.

Cross a shark with a parrot and what do you get?
   A bird that talks your ear off!

A father owl told his son, "It's not what you know that counts—it's WHOOOO you know."

55

One book company publishes detective stores as well as books about owls. You might say they specialize in WHOOO done-its.

Where do tough chickens come from?
  Hard-boiled eggs.

Why did the hens complain?
  They were sick of working for chicken feed.

One hen even tried to run away—she was tired of being all COOPED up.

A hungry pelican caught a large fish and said, "This sure fills the bill!"

Did you hear about the seagull that landed on a harbor buoy?
It was a case of BUOY meets GULL.

Confucius say, "Duck who fly upside down must quack up!"

Smart-alec ducks love to make *wise quacks*.

A duckling is a bird that grows down while it grows up.

Why do ducks often look so sad when they are preening their feathers?
They get down in the mouth.

Cross a parrot with a centipede and what do you get?
A walkie talkie!

What do birds like to watch on television?
The feather forecast.

What did the bird say to the miser?
Cheep! Cheep!

What's the difference between a crow with one wing and a crow with two wings?

A difference of a pinion.

How did the chicken farmer get up in the morning?

He had an alarm cluck.

What happened to the pelican who stuck his head into the wall socket?

He was given an electric bill.

Why are birds poor?

Because money doesn't grow on trees.

A tern once shared a fish it had caught with another tern. As a result the two terns became great friends. This story illustrates an old saying: *ONE GOOD TERN DESERVES ANOTHER*.

Icarus was a SOAR loser.

What kind of geese are found in Portugal?
  Portu-geese.

Did you hear about the sick bird who had to go to the hospital for special tweetment?

What bird can't be trusted?
  A stool pigeon.

Cross a puppy with a chicken and what do you get?
  Pooched eggs.

Which bird was allowed to stay at the round table with King Arthur?
  The knightingale.

What happened to the newly-hatched egg?
  It chickened out.

What do you get if you cross a chicken with a guitar?
A hen that makes music when you pluck it.

What happened to the canary that got caught in the lawn mower?
It wound up as shredded tweet.

What do birds love to eat for a snack?
Corn cheeps.

Which geometric figure is like a runaway parrot?
A polygon (polly gone).

Teacher: Use the word POLITICS in a sentence.
Student: Our pet parrot swallowed a watch and now my *polly ticks*.

Some birds of prey can be very HAWKward.

Did you hear about the turkey farmer? He's just installed a GOBBLEstone driveway.

The hen told her son—"If your father could see you now he'd turn over in his gravy."

Who conquered part of the world, laying eggs wherever he went?

Attila the Hen.

Why is it a waste of time to hold a party for chickens?

'Cause it's hard to make hens meet.

Knight School

The knights of old were expert duellers—they were pretty FENCY fellows.

He: I read that all the members of King Arthur's Round Table had insomnia.
She: Wow—that's what I call having a lot of sleepless knights.

Why were Medieval times called the Dark Ages?
  Because in those days there were so many knights.

When the king needed a new man to take charge of the gallows what kind of person did he look for?
Someone who easily got the HANG of things.

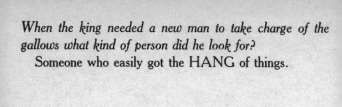

As the prisoner was being taken to the torture chamber to be put on the rack, he remarked, "Oh dear—it looks as though I'll be here for a long stretch."

What did the wife of Sir Galahad always wear to bed?
A knightgown.

What's the favorite drink of queens?
Royaltea.

When is a piece of wood like a king?
  When it's made into a ruler.

Who was known as the podiatrist king?
  William the Corncurer.

How did King Arthur get across the ditch that surrounded his castle?
  He took a moator boat.

Which of the knight's coats has the most sleeves?
  His coat of armor.

What did the king weigh before leaving harbor?
  Anchor.

Why are knights in training like coal in a mine?
  Because they're so often drilled.

Where did Sir Lancelot study?
  In knight school.

Why did knights use swords?
  They had a duel purpose.

A nobleman who owned several castles had to sell all his property. After that he became bitter and rude. You might say he lost all his MANORS.

Robin Hood was lucky to ride off alive after the King's knights fired at him. You could say he had an ARROW escape.

Which English king had a heart transplant from an animal?
   Richard the Lionheart.

What did the princess say to the knight when she saw a dragon?
   "Don't just stand there—SLAY something!"

Which one of King Arthur's knights was always telling jokes?
   Sir Laughalot.

Why did Henry VIII have so many wives?
   He liked to go chopping.

What was Sir Lancelot's name when he was small?
   Sir Lance-a-little.

How did the jester feel when he heard he would be hanged?
   All choked up!

Why didn't the maiden want to date Sir Lancelot?
   She considered him a fly-by-knight.

What did Sir Lancelot's wife do before he went to sleep?
   She kissed him goodKNIGHT.

Why did Sir Lancelot wake up screaming?
   He had a terrible KNIGHTmare.

In Medieval times burning torches brightened up the dark passages of the castles. You might say they were the first KNIGHT-lights.

The following words were engraved on a knight's tombstone:
   Here lies Sir John, ye knight of old, interred with his armor shining. MAY HE RUST IN PEACE.

Who guarded the castle after midnight?
   The knight watchman.

Why was the king's son always crying?

It was natural—after all, he was the Prince of Wails!

What did the executioner with the sword tell the accused man?

"Don't be nervous—it'll be over in necks to no time."

Why was the queen unhappy with the new minstrel and his instrument?

She was sick of listening to lyres.

What kind of fish do knights prefer?

SWORD fish.

Why do dragons sleep during the day?
   So they can fight knights.

Why did the princess take a ruler to bed?
   She wanted to see how long she slept.

Why is a champion tennis player like the kings of old?
   They both rule the courts.

What made Sir Lancelot happy?
   Taking the knight off.

Royalty can often be pretty empressive.

What did the queen say to the king?
    "Darling—I think I'm regnant."

What did the king wear when he was crowned?
    A REIGN-coat.

What happened to the first chair made for the king?
    It was throne out.

I've Been Aching To Meet You

When is dental surgery funny?
When it leaves the patient in stitches.

Why do most people think that dentists are artistic?
Because they're good at drawing teeth.

"Do you like your dentist?"
"No, he's a real BORE!"

Did you hear about the dentist who married a manicurist?
   They've been fighting tooth and nail ever since.

My dentist has no windows in his office. That's why they call him a PANEless dentist.

"Why did you punch the dentist?"
   "He got on my nerves."

My father always wanted to be a dentist, but he didn't have enough pull!

Our neighbor used to be a dentist but he had to quit—he couldn't stand the grind.

When a dentist makes a mistake it's acciDENTAL.

How do we know that all dentists are sad?
Because they always look down-in-the-mouth.

A man yelled, "This toothache of mine is driving me to extraction!"

How did the nervous carpenter break his teeth?
He bit his nails.

The old man's teeth are like stars—they come out at night.

One dentist has a sign outside his office which reads: FILL-ING STATION.

What did the new patient say to the dentist?
    "I've been aching to meet you!"

The dentist was sworn in at the trial and asked, "Do you swear to tell the tooth, the whole tooth and nothing but the tooth?"

What did they call a dentist in the days of the Wild West?
    A gum-slinger.

How would you describe going to the dentist?
    It's a drilling experience.

An osteopath is one doctor who makes no bones about his profession.

Patient: I have a severe headache.
Doctor: It's all in your mind.

A surgeon was operating on a patient when all of a sudden another doctor ran into the operating room and asked, "May I cut in?"

Most pediatricians are people who have little patients (patience).

An orthopedic surgeon is quite lucky—he gets all the breaks!

"Doctor, doctor—I'm breaking out all over in red spots."
"Don't make such rash statements."

"Doctor, doctor—I feel like a spoon."
"Sit right down and don't stir!"

"I don't want you to stitch me up," said the patient to the doctor.
"Suture self," came the answer.

There's one cardiologist who always operates on his patients near a large chimney—he believes in *open-hearth* surgery.

What do you call a building that houses lots of opticians' offices?
A site for sore eyes.

What kind of man is an optician?
   A man of vision.

A psychiatrist graduated from school at the head of his class.

A podiatrist graduated from medical college at the foot of his class.

My brother has had a cough for seven days. The doctor says not to worry—it's just a *wee cold*.

St. Peter asked the latest arrival, "How did you get here?"
   "Flu," was the answer.

Sneezing is much achoooo about nothing.

"What happened to your leg?" asked the wife anxiously.
"I fractured my ankle," said the husband LIMPLY.

When the hunter became sick in Africa, a local tribesman asked, "Witch doctor would you like to see?"

Here's a warning for people who have a smoker's cough:
IT ISN'T THE COUGH THAT CARRIES YOU OFF
IT'S THE COFFIN THEY CARRY YOU OFF IN.

An Australian tourist was run over in London and taken to a hospital. "Was I brought here to die?" he asked when he gained consciousness.

"Oh, no," answered the orderly, "you were brought here *yesterdie*."

What can happen if you watch too many Mickey Mouse cartoons?

You can get Disney spells.

I'm glad my electrocardiogram is normal, said the patient whole-heartedly.

When the operation was finally completed, the woman said, "I'm Gladys all over."

What was wrong with King Midas?
   He had a gilt complex.

Did you hear about the man who takes care of the cemetery?
   He's in the hospital in GRAVE condition.

Where is the nose located?
   In the scenter of the face.

Did you hear about the two blood cells that met and loved in vein?

Hit and Run

First Arab: How do you like traveling by flying carpet?
Second Arab: It's a RUGGED experience.

Why is Tibet the noisiest country in the world?
  Because wherever you go it's YAK, YAK, YAK!

Londoners must be the most ignorant of the Englishmen—
after all, it's in London where the population's so dense.

What was Dr. Jekyll's favorite game as a little boy?
  Hyde-and-seek.

There are many people with the names of Wing and Wong in China. In fact, many people refuse to use the telephone for fear that they'll Wing the Wong number.

Here's the latest Mexican weather report—chile today, hot tamale.

What do you call a tavern in Alaska?
   A polar bar.

Wife: I saw a giant rat on the oven, but when I went for the gun he ran away.
Husband: Did you try to shoot at him?
Wife: No—he was out of my range.

"Do you know how to get to Nevada?"
"I haven't the Vegas idea."

Who was Mexico's most famous fat man?
Pauncho Villa.

What do Chinese lumberjacks use to fell trees?
Chopsticks (what else?).

In China's port cities, mail is delivered by boat. You might
say it's all JUNK mail.

"My stallion's gone wild," he said hoarsely."

The Russian man named Rudolf looked out the window and said it was raining. His wife looked out the window and said it was snowing, to which her husband replied "Rudolf the Red knows rain, dear."

Adam and Eve could never gamble—after all, their pair o' dice was taken away from them.

What country is best to buy men's neckwear?
   Thailand (Tieland).

Two thirsty men without a thing to drink were crawling across the desert. One turned to the other and gasped, "Water we going to do?"

A girl met a boy named Arthur and took him home to meet her family. Her sister liked him very much and asked, "Arthur any more at home like you?"

What did Atlas' girlfriend say when no one was around?
    "Atlas we're alone."

A girl was drinking tea and reading *The Canterbury Tales* when her mother asked, "What have to you got there?"
    The girl answered, "Just my cup and Chaucer."

Most parents can't wait for New Year's Eve—it gives them some relief from the Christmas holly daze.

*When a farmer gave his friend a special milking pail, the
friend gave him back a cow. Why?*
Because one good urn deserves an udder.

How do you use an Egyptian doorbell?
Toot-and-come-in.

Did you read about the accident at the army camp?
A jeep ran over a popcorn box and killed two kernels!

What might you send to a man who is searching for oil?
A get-*WELL* card.

Did you hear about the timid stone whose only ambition
in life was to become a little boulder (bolder)?

During the Olympics a Danish skier injured himself—it was a slalom occasion.

The mold out of which good skiers are cast is usually plaster of Paris.

Skiing's a great sport—people are known to go skiing for hours ON END!

Dad thought he'd take up skiing, then he let it slide.

Any kid can be a basketball star when he grows up and up and up!

Of all sports basketball attracts the highest type of kid.

There's no such thing as a quiet game of tennis—every player has to raise a racket.

Getting athlete's foot after losing a tough tennis match could be described as the agony of defeet (defeat).

The coach at a tennis club gave lessons. He had a sign on the bulletin board which read: FIRST COME, FIRST SERVE.

Did you hear about the retired boxer who gave up his job as a masseur? He didn't like pulling paunches.

Skier—a person who jumps to contusions.

Fisherman's motto: LET'S GET THE SHOW ON THE ROD.

A boxer who gets beat up in a fight is usually a sore loser.

He was a colorful boxer—black and blue all over!

Prize-fighter—a man who makes money hand over fist.

One boxer celebrates his birthday with a great deal of FISTivity.

A successful fighter always has to consider the *rights* of others.

A prize-fighter is a man who believes it's better to give than to receive.

One kid is absolutely crazy about riding his bicycle—does that make him a cycle-path?

The goalie on a soccer team was nicknamed Cinderella—because he always missed the ball!

Bowlers are people who thoroughly enjoy their sport—they always have a ball.

Badminton is a game for the birdies.

Table tennis is known as the sport of pings.

Fencing—the art of missing the point.

Mountaineer—somebody who starts at the bottom and works his way up.

When is baseball a crime?
    When it's hit and run.

Dad says that bowling is a sport that's right down his alley.

Why is Cinderella a rotten soccer player?
    Because she has a pumpkin for a coach.

The boat race began and the wife of one of the boat owners shouted, "Yachts of luck!"

A bowling alley is a place where, even if it's noisy, you can still hear a pin drop.

Why did the jockey's wife divorce him?
  He horsed around too much.

My father loves to go fishing—he's a FINatic!

Why did one man become a wrestler?
  It was a sport which really grabbed him.

The members of a bicycle club are voting today for a new
SPOKESman.

Why did the man invent soccer?
  He got a kick out of it.

People who buy jogging machines get a run for their money.

For a new father, the son always shines.

Siamese twins are an exception to the rule that two heads are better than one.

What's a maternity ward?
  A BAWL-room.

Some people think of twins as a double take.

What are newly-hatched termites called?
  Babes in the wood.

Son: What's an umbilical cord?
Father: The site of a navel operation.

There's nothing like having a baby to make you realize it's a CHANGING world.

Did you read about the snake who gave birth to a bouncing baby boa?

Infant care has to be learned from the BOTTOM up!

They say that having a baby takes a lot out of a mother!

Twins usually get along well because they started off as *womb-mates*.

What do you call a woman who has more than ten children?
  Stork-raving mad!

Two cans of paint got married. Soon after, the bride whispered to the groom, "Darling, I think I'm pigment."

Siamese twins have a strong family THAI.

Why is an old car like a baby?
   Because it never goes anywhere without a rattle.

What did the electrician's wife say when he came home after midnight?
   "Wire you insulate?"

How do you make anti-freeze?
   Hide her nightie.

What did the Eskimo wife say to her husband when he finished building the igloo?
   "What an ice little house."

"How do you like my new sculpture?"
"It's marbleous!"

Shopkeeper: What kind of nuts would you like?
Customer: Cashew.
Shopkeeper: Bless you—now what kind of nuts would you like?

What kind of motorbike would a Japanese comedian purchase?
A Yama-ha-ha.

The short-haired captain of a ship was forced to make reductions in staff. You might say he had a CREW cut.

What was barbed wire first used for?
  DEFENCE.

Did the inventor of the packaging machine make money?
  I'll say—he made a bundle.

Did you hear about the convention of nudists? Probably not—they got little coverage.

A large shipment of umbrellas was sent from London to New York—they were mailed by *parasol* post.

What happened to the man who first invented the boomerang?
  Last I heard he was trying for a comeback.

Straw hats used to be in style many years ago—that's when they were in their hay day.

When the executioner needed a new axe, he put it on his *chopping* list.

Did you know that adding machines are so popular they're beginning to multiply?

Pogo sticks can make people jumpy.

A bathing beauty is a girl worth *wading* for.

Dad just rented a dog kennel—he got it on a thirty-year *leash.*

One reporter was very happy to cover the story of the opening of a new ice cream factory. He got a big scoop!

Mary: High heels will soon be going out of fashion.
Friend: Too bad—that's going to be a big letdown.

Where can you see the building plans for a beer factory?
  On a brew-print.

What is Australian beer made from?
  Kangaroo hops.

When's the best day for twins to be born?
   Two's-day.

"My husband keeps getting holes in his socks," a woman complained. "Being married to him is just one darned thing after another."

A new type of circuit breaker has been invented, but many people reFUSE to use it.

Which is the most appropriate day of the week to use tanning oil?
   SUNday.

How did home owners feel when wrought iron was first used for building fences?
Very GRATEful.

How do you enter a houseboat?
Just BARGE in!

A sign on a garbage truck read: ALWAYS AT YOUR DISPOSAL.

What do you call a quick path through a berry patch?
A strawberry shortcut.

When mom first saw gray in her hair, she thought she'd dye!

"What do you think of flying lighter-than-air craft?"
  "As far as I'm concerned, it's a lot of balloony."

One old lady put wheels on her rocking chair because she wanted to rock and roll!

They say that Cupid's aim is excellent, but he still makes a lot of Mrs.

What's the dirtiest part of a ship?
  The officers' mess.

Accidents will happen, remarked Captain Hook, *off-handedly*.

Card-playing is no longer allowed on U.S. naval ships. You might say that the boats have lost their decks.

One teenage boy had two girlfriends—Kate and Edith. His father had a heart-to-heart talk with him and said, "Son, you can't have your Kate and Edith too."

Why did the parents call their only child Margarine? Because they didn't have any but'er.

There's one kid who's hoping for a lucky stroke—his rich uncle's!

Miser—a man who lets the rest of the world go buy.

There are two classes of people—the have-nots and the have-yachts.

My dad keeps wondering: Is there life after debt?

That money talks, I'll not deny
I heard it once, it said "Goodbye."

Our neighbors have struck it rich and have become snobs.
  Now they're moving to SNUBurbia.

Have you heard about the undertakers? They're on strike demanding a LIVING wage!

My mom is working for a good cause—'cause she needs money!

An Arab oil millionaire has money to burn!

If money talks, then credit cards use sign language.

How did the Vikings send each other messages?
  By Norse code.

Did you hear about the man and woman who got stuck in a revolving door together? They're still going around with each other.

Snappy Answers

Cross a math teacher with a crab and what do you get?
  Snappy answers!

What are metrics?
  A system of measures which is a FEET to understand.

Why was the geometry teacher boring?
  He was a square and he talked in circles.

What's the best way to pass a geometry test?
  Know all the angles.

Did you hear what happened to the plants in the math room?
  They grew square roots!

Which Englishman discovered the circle?
  Sir Cumference.

Why is a baby the least important member of a family?
  Because it doesn't count.

Why are waiters especially good at arithmetic?
  Because they know their tables.

He: Have you heard the joke about pocket calculators?
She: No
He: It figures.

Which English king enjoyed doing fractions?
  Henry the Eighth.

A kindergarten teacher is someone who knows how to make little things count.

To a math teacher, fractions speak louder than words.

Science teacher: The fleas we find on domestic pets are small, dark-colored pests.

Little Anna: I thought they were white.

Science teacher: Where did you get that idea?

Little Anna: From the poem, "Mary had a little lamb, its FLEAS was white as snow . . ."

Teacher: What can you tell me about the salivary glands?

Student: Not much—they're very secretive.

Teacher: Can you tell the class what nationality Napoleon was?

Student: Course I can.

Teacher: Correct.

Why was the teacher like a man with one eye?
Because he had a vacancy for one pupil.

A teacher was reading the *Canterbury Tales* to his class. When he noticed one student sleeping, the teacher was so mad he threw the book at the boy.

"What was that?" asked the startled student.

The teacher answered, "A flying Chaucer."

Teacher: Give me a sentence containing the word "avenue."

Student: My mom is about to give birth and soon I'll *avenue* brother or sister.

Sister: Why are you taking that toy car to school?

Brother: To drive my teacher up the wall!

Teacher: Use the word "climate" in a sentence.

Student: The mountain was so steep, I couldn't climate.

116

Billy: How did you feel after the teacher spanked you?
Fred: Absolutely *whacked*!

Why was the cross-eyed teacher fired?
  Because she had no control over her pupils.

My dad suffers from a low-grade infection—every time he sees my report card he feels sick!

Student: I'm sorry I'm late, but I sprained my ankle.
Teacher: That's a lame excuse!

A famous teacher of literature was sick. He received a get-well card which began, "Dear ill literate . . ."

Teacher: How do you spell weather?

Student: W-e-t-t-t-e-r.

Teacher: That's the worst spell of weather we've ever had.

STAY IN SCHOOL AND BE UP TO KNOW GOOD!

My friend is so stupid he thinks an autobiography is a history of cars.

What did the horse get on his report card?
  Straight hays.

Why are teachers so special?
  Well, after all, they're in a class of their own.

Little Jimmy thinks the oldest piece of furniture in the world is the multiplication table!

Teacher: Can you tell me anything about the Iron Age?
Student: I'm afraid I'm a bit rusty on the subject.

Teacher: If the ruler of Russia was called the czar, and his wife was called the czarina, what were his children called?
Student: Czardines.

Why did the history teacher keep on all the lights?
    Because his class was so dim!

The teacher told her class "Color your pictures with any color you want—hue can have your choice."

Teacher: Do we get fur from a grizzly bear?
Student: Yes, as fur as possible!

Father: How are your science grades?
Daughter: I'm afraid they're under water
Father: What is that supposed to mean?
Daughter: They're below C level.

"When rain falls, does it ever rise again?" asked the science teacher.
   "Yes sir."
   "When?"
   "In DEW time."

Jane handed in her homework and the teacher said, "You were supposed to write a three-page report about cows and milk, but you've only handed in half a page." To this Jane answered, "That's because I decided to write about CONDENSED milk."

Hogwash

How does an octopus go into battle?
  Well-armed!

Cross a bee with chopped meat and what do you get?
  A HUMburger.

How do rabbits keep their fur so nice and clean?
  They use a HAREbrush.

Why is a pig unique from a medical point of view?
   Because you have to kill him before you cure him.

What do you say when you bump into a dolphin?
   Tell him you didn't do it on porpoise.

How did young dinosaurs pass their exams?
   With extinction.

What did the hungry donkey say when he discovered there were only thistles to eat?
   "Thisle have to do!"

What is horse sense?
   It's just stable thinking.

What has large antlers and wears white gloves?
  Mickey Moose.

Can you get fur from a snake?
  Yes, as fur as possible.

What do you give a sick rabbit?
  A hoperation.

What is a zebra?
  A horse behind bars.

What's the best year for kangaroos?
  A leap year.

What do termites do when they want to relax?
  Take a coffee-table break.

Did you hear about the two rabbits that got married?
  After the ceremony they went on a bunnymoon!

What is it called when pigs do their laundry?
  Hogwash!

What happens to a rabbit when it gets very cross?
  It gets hoppin' mad!

What did the rabbit want to do when it grew up?
  He wanted to join the hare force.

Cross a flea with a rabbit and what do you get?
  Bugs Bunny.

What did the little skunk want to be when he grew up?
  A big stinker!

Why was the horse called a hot-head?
  Because it had a blaze on its forehead.

Why did the farmer raise bees?
  He liked to keep buzzy.

What did the buck say to the doe?
  "Let's have a little fawn."

Why does a frog have more lives than a cat?
   A cat has nine lives, but a frog croaks every night.

What do you call a young moth that cries when it's spanked?
   A moth bawl.

What do you call a fast duck?
   A quick quack.

What did the skunk say when the wind suddenly changed direction?
   "It all comes back to me now."

How do you make a baby snake cry?
   Take away its rattle.

How do rabbits travel?
  By hareplane.

Operating a rabbit farm is said to be a *hare-raising* experience!

Baby firebug: I feel hot.
Mother firebug: That's just glowing pains.

If a whale gave birth to a boy and a girl, what relation would they be?
  Blubber and sister.

In the days before automobiles, when people traveled by horse and buggy, we had a STABLE economy.

What did the ram say to his girlfriend to show he was a gentlemen?
"After ewe."

Girl goat to boy goat: "I'll go out with you, but don't try to kid me."

What kind of animal weighs over a thousand pounds and wears flowers in his hair?
A HIPPIEpotamus.

What famous motto do otters live by?
DO UNTO OTTERS AS YOU WOULD HAVE OTTERS DO UNTO YOU.

What kind of accommodation might a homeless piglet look for?
   A small apartment to runt.

What an arrogant insect—it's a COCKY-roach!

Goats have bad manners—they're always butting in!

What might you call a squirrel's nest?
   A nutcracker suite.

Did you hear about the two frogs that got married and lived HOPPILY ever after?

One turtle with a great memory told another, "I have turtle recall."

Why did the giant sea mammal look so glum?
  It wasn't feeling very whale.

Where do you put a herd of pigs?
  In a PORKING lot.

How did the frog feel?
  Very hoppy.

First pig: I never sausage heat.
Second pig: It's true—I'm almost bacon.

How do you hire a horse?
   Put a brick under each leg.

What did the pig say when the chef cut off his tail?
   This is the end of me.

Did you hear about the two silkworms that were competing against each other? The ended up in a tie!

When one mouse was drowning, what did his friend do?
   Gave him mouse-to-mouse resuscitation.

Why was the pony unhappy?
   Every time it wanted something, its mother would say, "Neigh."

When the pony was sick where was he taken?
   To the horse-pital.

Why doesn't it cost very much to feed a horse?
   Because a horse eats best when it doesn't have a bit in
   its mouth.

What might you title a funny book about dogs?
   The Reader's Dogjest.

What's another name for a dog sled?
   A polar coaster.

What's another name for a dog kennel?
   A used CUR lot.

A dog died and on his tombstone was engraved:
HERE LIES ROVER MY FAITHFUL DOG.
HE NEVER MET A MAN HE DIDN'T LICK.

Why did the dog keep barking after it was fed?
   He was still hungry and wanted a second yelping.

News flash: Snoopy has just handed in his resignation—
apparently, he's tired of working for *Peanuts*.

The woman gave her dog something to chew on, saying
"*Bone* appetit."

The intelligent dog went to college and graduated with a DOG-torate degree.

What did the angry bulldog say to his friend?
   "I've got a bone to pug with you."

Did you hear about the dog that went to the flea circus?
   He stole the show.

The cocker spaniel was exhausted; in fact he was DOG-tired.

The two young canines felt very emotional about each other, but was it just a case of puppy love?

What kind of dog loves to have a bath ten times a day?
 A SHAMPOODLE.

To a dog, the best things in life are FLEA!

What does every mother flea want?
 To see her children go to the dogs.

The first flea circus started from *scratch!*

How do you begin a flea race?
 Just say, "One, two, *flea*—GO!"

Did you hear about the talented dog who was able to sing a *bark* (Bach) cantata?

What happened when the poodle's owner got mad at her?
   She was in the doghouse.

When must a dog never yelp?
   When it's in a no-barking zone.

News flash: The first all-white Dalmation has just been spotted.

There are always scores of dogs in the park during the afternoon.
   I try not to go there during PEKE hours.

What did the dog say when it sat on some sandpaper?
  'Ruff!'

A cat is the one animal that never cries over spilled milk.

What happened when the cat entered the milk-drinking competition?
  It won by six laps.

Why was the cat so small?
  It was brought up on condensed milk.

Did you know that New York has the highest number of cats PURR capita?

Show me a cat that just ate a lemon, and I'll show you a sour puss!

Did you hear about the cat that ate a pound of cheese, then waited for a mouse with BAITED breath?

I'm learning to break into homes—a cat burglar's teaching MEOW.

What did the cat shout when it was put in prison?
"Let meowt of here!"

Arab cats come from the PURRsian Gulf.

Where do cats go for a vacation?
  Meowmi Beach.

Cross a Chinese cat with an alley cat, and you'll wind up with a Peking Tom.

What cat became a famous composer of operas?
  PUSSini.

First cat: You seem very interested in tennis.
Second cat: Not really, it's just that my father's in the racket.

Did you hear about the kitten that fell into the Xerox machine and became a copycat?

What do you call a cat that knows about medicine?
   A first-aid KIT.

What do they call big African cats?
   FELIONS.

An African cat escaped from the zoo—the story made the headLIONS.

One owner yelled at his cat and hurt her *felines* (feelings).

Did you hear about the leopard who kept himself very, very clean?
   He was spotless!

Are young religious cats sent for KITTYCHISM lessons?

Why did the new mother cat put her babies in the garbage can?

She saw a sign which read: PLACE YOUR LIT-
TER HERE.

When cats die, do they go to PURRgatory?

When the ape started work at his new job his boss told
him, "Now just behave yourself, and don't try any monkey
business."

What do monkeys sing during a thunderstorm?
   "I'm swingin' in the rain . . ."

What do you call a murderous ape?
   A killa gorilla.

When the ape won the boxing title he became the new CHIMPion of the world.

The ape was sick and tired—you might say he wasn't feeling up to scratch!

What was wrong with one of the apes that over-ate?
   He was going bananas!

What do you call a religious ape?
   A MONKey.

What ape is like a citrus fruit?
   An ORANGE-utang.

Which apes are Irish?
   O'rangutangs.

Did you read about the chimp that went in for yoga and finished up as a monkey puzzle?

What ape fries potatoes in the zoo?
   A chip-monkey.

The gorilla at the zoo was pregnant, and all the workers were making bets on what sex the infant would be. On the day of the delivery, the vet announced, "It's a GIRLilla!"

What ape was a famous American pioneer?
  Daniel Baboone.

What ape was the first emperor of France?
  Napoleon Baboonaparte.

What do you call an ape that drinks twenty cups of hot chocolate a day?
  A Cocoa-nut.

What did the chimp say when he heard his sister had just given birth?

"Well I'll be a monkey's uncle!"

Name the kind of apes that talk a lot.

Blab-boons.

When a female gorilla is in the kitchen, what does she wear?

An APE-ron.

Why was the gorilla rushed to the hospital?

Because he had APE-pendicitis.

How do gorillas show they like a performer?

With loud APE-plause.

What do you call a happy ape?
   A GAYrilla.

What tree can a gorilla hold in its hands?
   A palm tree.

What do you say to gorillas before you begin a meal with them?
   Bon APEtit.

Name the Chinese gorilla who became famous in pictures.
   King Wong.

Why do apes wear banana skins on their feet?
   They make very good slippers.

How do you measure the waist of a gorilla?
   With a T-APE measure.

What's big and hairy, and flies at over a thousand miles an hours?
   King Kong-corde.

What did the pregnant ape say to her friend?
   "Soon I'm going to be a MOM-key."

Did you know that the gorilla Sitting Bull was an APE-ache Indian?

Monstrous Mirth

News flash: King Kong has just joined the army—he's hoping to learn about GORILLA warfare.

Did you hear about the two cyclops who had a terrible fight because they couldn't see eye-to-eye?

What does the Invisible Man call his father and mother?
Transparents.

The boss told his secretary, "Tell the Invisible Man I can't see him right now."

When the boy monster met the girl monster their hearts began to throb—it was love at first fright!

Why was the witch thrown out of school?
  She couldn't learn to spell.

Did you hear about all the witches who got together and formed a union?
  They started demanding *sweeping* reforms.

One poor monster had to be rushed to the hospital for an emergency operation—she had her GHOULstones removed.

The werewolf told the wolfman, "You're not looking well lately—in fact, you look like you're going to the dogs!"

Did you hear about the exhausted zombie who felt dead on his feet?

The monster snowman wasn't feeling too well. In fact he was feeling *abominable*.

What's the first thing a ghost does when it gets into a car?
  It fastens its sheet-belt.

Name the skeleton that was Emperor of France.
  Napoleon Bone-apart.

Did you hear about the monster that went to an astrologer to hear his HORRORscope?

How far did the ghost travel?
  From ghost to ghost.

Baron Frankenstein was a lonely man until he learned how to make friends.

When King Kong was insulted, what did he demand?
  An ape-ology.

What do you call a movie about spies starring King Kong?
  A gorilla thrilla.

Why was the ghost fined?
   He was haunting without a license.

What do you call a wizard who moves through the air like a bird?
   A flying sorcerer.

Why did Dracula go to the dentist?
   To improve his bite.

Do you know what vampire sailors call their ships?
   Blood vessels.

Why is it easy to fool vampires?
   Because they're known to be suckers.

What do monster children enjoy eating on a hot day?
   Ice SCREAM!

Dracula once became lost while driving on a small road—
he was searching for the main artery!

You can always trust a mummy. They know how to keep
things under wraps.

There's one skeleton who's very fussy when it comes to
eating. He refuses to eat off paper plates and will only use
BONE china.

What's the best present to give a witch for Christmas?
A charm bracelet.

One monster magazine always had a picture of a beauty on the front—she's called the *cover ghoul*.

A skeleton went to the ball and looked very sad. A witch came over and asked, "Why are you looking so unhappy?"
The skeleton answered, "Because I have no BODY to dance with."

When the sorceress lost her broom, how did she get back home?
She had to witch-hike.

What do sorceresses like to eat?
   Sandwitches.

Beware of beautiful witches——they'll sweep you right off your feet.

Why was the mother ghost worried about her son?
   Because he seemed to be in such good spirits all the time.

What do you call a skeleton that sleeps all day and refuses to work?
   A real lazy-bones.

What does a ghost wear when it has poor eyesight?
   Spooktacles.

Ghost: I'd like a gin and tonic please.
Bartender: Sorry—no spirits served here.

Ghosts are cowards—they've got no *guts*!

When monsters travel, they always use American Scarelines.

What did the ghost coach tell his ghost football players?
   "We need more team spirit!"

Poor Dracula—he's always accused of being a *pain-in-the-neck*!

Did you hear that Dracula had to be put in an insane asylum?
Apparently, he went completely batty!

What's the favorite food of ghosts?
Taboooli!

What do you call a pig that turns into a bat at night and sucks blood?
A hampire.

Missionary: Do you like beans?
Cannibal: Very much.
Missionary: What kind of beans do you prefer?
Cannibal: Human bein's!

The cannibal told the waitress: "I'd like to order some soup with a full-bodied flavor!"

"No cannibal will ever eat me," said the missionary, "after all, you can't keep a good man down."

Cannibal: We've just captured an actor.
Chief: That's wonderful news—I was just in the mood for a thick HAM sandwich.

The cannibal chief had a Chinese wife who tried never to waste any food. Whenever there were any leftovers, she made CHAP suey.

Have you heard about the hippie cannibal who ate three squares a day?

There's one cannibal who's looking forward to becoming a detective so he can GRILL all the suspects!

Why didn't the cannibals boil missionary Tuck?
    Because he was a friar.

It was an old missionary who gave the tribe of cannibals their first *taste* of Christianity.

First cannibal: How do you know our new missionary has been eaten?
Second cannibal: I've got inside information.

What did the cannibal chief tell his daughter?
   "Soon you'll be old enough to marry—we've got to start looking for an EDIBLE young bachelor."

For breakfast you'll find most cannibals enjoying a cup of steaming hot coffee with buttered *host*!

What did the missionary say when the cannibals put him in the cooking pot?
   "At least you'll get a taste of religion."

Good Turns

The circus is in town—all children must be accompanied by *money* and daddy.

The two-headed man at the circus has just gone on strike.
  He wants more money because he has an extra mouth to feed.

Tightrope walkers are said to be *high-strung* people.

Why did the old tightrope walker decide to retire?
   His performance began to fall off!

What did the trampoline artist say to his friend?
   "Even when I'm not feeling well, I always manage to bounce right back."

Why did the sword swallower consider leaving the circus?
   He was fed up to the hilt!

"I hear the sword swallower has just quit."
   "That's correct—the boss wanted him to take a CUT!"

Why did the old sword swallower swallow an umbrella?
   He knew that he'd soon be retiring, so he wanted to put something away for a rainy day.

Why couldn't the dwarf lend the giant $10?
　Because he was very short.

Acrobats are nice people to know—they're always doing such good turns.

What purrs in the circus when it swings?
　An Acro-cat.

Acrobats are people who can turn a flop into a success!

A trapeze artist is a person who easily gets the hang of things.

What happened to the midget who applied for a job at the circus?

He was put on a short list.

Why is a traveling circus like a raging fire?

Because the heat is in tents. (*intense*)

Andrea: I went to the circus and had five rides on the carousel.

Ivan: Wow! You really get around!

What did the boss tell the human cannonball?

"You're fired!"

What became of the rubber man?
He was caught stealing, so they sent him to jail for a long stretch.

Why couldn't the great Houdini come to the phone?
He was all tied up at the time.

Why did the elephants want to run away from the circus?
They were tired of working for peanuts.

Congratulations are in order for the rubber man—he's just become the father of a bouncing baby boy!

A man applied for a job at the circus to become a human cannonball.

The manager said, "We're looking for someone of just the right caliber."

Why are tightrope walkers like bookkeepers?
Because they know how to balance.

Why is waiting on the telephone like doing a trapeze act?
Because you have to hang on.

What does an acrobat have in common with a whisky glass?
They're both tumblers.

Contortionists are thrifty people—they certainly know how to make both ends meet.

How can you discover the tightrope walker's secret?
  By tapping his wire.

Why is a clown like an operation?
  Both leave you in stitches.

"Who was Captain Kidd?"
  "He was a contortionist."
  "What do you mean he was a contortionist?"
  "I read that he often sat on his chest."

A pony at the circus had a sore throat. The trainer said he was just a little HORSE!

What season is it when the circus features its trampoline artist?
   Springtime.

The ringmaster told the audience, "We regret to announce that the Invisible Man will not be seen tonight."

What happened to the man who worked as a human cannonball at the circus?
   He was discharged.

There was one acrobat who was good-natured—he'd bend over backwards to help you.

One world-renowned violinist said that when he was just a little boy he became involved in music up to his chin.

I know one harpist—he's a pretty plucky fellow.

Interviewer: Why did you choose to play trombone?
Musician: Because it was the only instrument on which I could get anywhere by simply letting things slide.

Never trust a trumpeter—he's a *toot-timer*.

People who play woodwind instruments are said to have a lot of SAX appeal.

Organist—a musician with many pipe dreams

When a friend asked Bach to lend him some money, the great composer replied, "I'm sorry, but I'm baroque."

Did you hear about the thief who robbed the music store and ran off with the LUTE?

Pianos are such noble instruments—they're either upright or grand.

Banging together the big brass plates in an orchestra is not as cymbal as it looks!

A sign on the door of a music shop read: COME IN—
PICK OUT A DRUM—THEN BEAT IT!

The owner of a music shop closed up for a short time and
hung out a sign which read: GONE CHOPIN, BE
BACH IN A MINUET.

Son: What's an organ grinder?
Father: That's a man who walks around with a chimp
on his shoulder.

OPERATIC music—the kind that goes in one aria and
out the other.

A soprano and a tenor from the same choir ended up
getting married.

You might say they met by CHANTS.

His mother egged him on to become an opera singer, and the audience egged him off!

What song did the opera singer sing at the funeral?
   "Oh what a beautiful mourning . . ."

Wagner was a man who was often accused of being an OPERAtunist.

Conductor—a man who is not afraid to face the music.

Opera critic—a person who gives the best jeers of his life to music.

One opera singer sang an aria as though she were sharp-raving mad.

She was so out-of-tune that she was given the off-key to the city!

Husband: Shall we sing an aria together?
Wife: Okay—let's DUET.

Singing in the tub is every man's bathright.

"If he's from Glasgow he's SCOT to be good."

When can you hear an organ recital?
When two musicians discuss their operations.

What do you call an assistant conductor?
  A band-aide.

The first music score was Mozart 5, Brahms 3.

What kind of music is written in bed?
  Sheet music.

The pianist searched all through the house complaining, "Who's Hadyn my Chopin Liszt?"

What do famous movie stars drive in?
  Os-CARS.

What might you call an unemployed movie star?
  A movie idle.

Why did the comedian's wife sue for divorce?
    She claimed her husband was always trying to joke her
    to death.

Interviewer: What is your favorite role?
Actor: Cheese and ham.

Moo York, Moo York!

What happened to the man who stole some milk?
   He was taken into custardy.

Why are bulls so noisy?
   It's because of their horns.

What cow speaks Russian?
   Ma's cow (Moscow).

What American city has lots of cows?
 Moo York.

What game do cows play?
 Mooosical chairs.

Cross a cow with a duck and what do you get?
 An animal that gives milk and quackers.

Milking cows is simple—any *jerk* can do it.

What cow discovered the New World?
 Christopher Cowlumbus.

There's one cow who comes from a high station in life—she's a member of the noBULLity.

How does a cow keep itself from being seen?
  It uses cowmooflage.

Calves love to ride on the COWrousel.

Bull: I've come across miles of pasture just to see you.
Cow: That sounds like a lot of bull to me.

When cows die, do they want to be CREAMated?

What do you get if you cross an octopus with a cow?
   An animal that can milk itself.

What do cows like to watch on TV?
   The mooos of the day.

What happens to cows after an earthquake?
   They give milk shakes.

What's the easiest way to count a large herd of cattle?
   Use a Cowculator.

Where do cows go for their vacation?
   Sunny Cowlifornia.

Jokes about cows are UDDER nonsense.

When's the best time to milk a cow?
  When she's in the moooood.

Why did the manager of the candy factory hire the farmer's daughter?
  He needed someone to milk chocolate.

Where do you get milk in the Sahara Desert?
  From the dromeDAIRY.

What do you call the boss of a dairy?
  The big cheese.

If two cows helped each other, would you call it COWoperation?

What do you get from a forgetful cow?
Milk of amnesia.

What kind of cows live in the far north?
Eskimooos.

Remember—if you sing to a cow, do it in the key of BEEF flat.

To a cow, no moos is good moos.

Did you hear about the cow that went dry?
   It was an UDDER failure.

Since the farmer found a WHEY to make money, he's doing much BUTTER.

Why do cows go to beaches?
   To tan their hides.

What famous beach do cows go to for holidays?
   Mooami Beach.

Production costs are very high in the dairy business. A lot of expenses are inCURD.

Where might you see a prehistoric cow?
  In a mooseum.

Where do cattle like to eat?
  At a COWfeteria.

How do cows send messages?
  By Moooose code.

One summer it was so hot, the farmer's cows gave evaporated milk!

One farmer feeds his cows money, hoping they'll give rich milk!

What caused a riot at the post office?
   A STAMP-ede.

Where do cows go for entertainment?
   To the Moooovies.

What kind of cattle are vagrants?
   Bum steers.

Why don't cows ever have money?
   Because farmers milk them dry.

What music do bulls prefer?
   COWlypso music.

To 'err is human—to give milk, bovine.

If the cow that jumped over the moon fought Taurus the bull, would it be called STEER wars?

What did the cow say to the bull that kept looking at her? "Stop STEERing at me!"

Cattle that cry are called steers with tears.

A cow awoke early one morning and remarked, "It's the start of anUDDER day."

Why did the cow go to the psychiatrist?
Because it had a fodder complex.

Many cattle are true BULLievers.

"Once a week I like to take a bath in milk."
"Pasteurized?"
"No—just up to my neck."

What did the bull sing to the cow?
"When I fall in love, it will be for heifer . . ."

What do you call a bovine from a backwoods area?
A hillBULLY.

Once there was a male bovine who became a famous cowboy outlaw—his name was BULLY the Kid.

What might you buy for a calf at an amusement park?
  A BULLoon.

Where do you take a baby cow to eat?
  To the CALFeteria.

How do cattle feel about the branding iron?
  Very impressed.

Gluttons for PUNishment

What happened when there was a fight at the seafood restaurant?

Two cod got battered.

Why can't anyone steal the Panama Canal?

Because it has too many locks.

Who's the main witness at a trial of a bank robber?

The teller.

Did you hear about the safecracker who decided to give the money back?

He was generous to a *vault!*

What type of robbery is the least dangerous?

Safe robbery.

Why did the pig thief get caught?

The pig squealed.

Why was the judge so exhausted when he returned home?

It had been a very *trying* day.

Why did the owner of a bar refuse to serve coal workers?
  He was afraid he might be charged with serving alcohol to miners (minors).

Why was the policeman hiding up a tree?
  He was a member of the Special Branch.

How does a rotten kid learn to get what he wants?
  By trial and terror!

When a counterfeiter was asked, "How's business?" what did he answer?
  "Forging ahead!"

Who was the famous cowboy who terrorized the seabed?
  Billy the squid.

What did the artist say when he was convicted of murder?
  "I didn't do it—I've been framed!"

One thief was allergic to jail. Every time he was put into a cell, he began to *break out*!

Did you hear about the hangman who found his job a laugh?
  He thought of himself as a *practical choker*!

Judge: Why did you steal all those nickels, dimes, and quarters?

Defendant: I wasn't feeling well, and I thought the *change* would do me good.

Did you hear about the kid who threatened to jump off a cliff?

It was only a *bluff.*

The gangster gave his wife a mink stole for her birthday. "Is it really a mink stole?" she asked. "I'm not certain if its genuine mink," answered the gangster, "but it definitely is STOLE!"

The murderer was given a suspended sentence—he was *hanged!*

A midget fortune-teller escaped from jail. Newspaper headlines read: "Small medium at large."

An old man grabbed a woman on the street, kissed her, then told her how beautiful she looked. He was arrested for *assault and flattery*.

Did you hear about the delinquent kid? He was always on his pest behavior.

The convicted murderer was waiting to hear his fate. Finally his lawyer came to tell him he would be hanged. The murderer commented, "No noose is good noose."

When the convicts at a prison put on a show, it was a CELL-out!

Why couldn't the judge be disturbed at dinner?
   Because his Honor was at steak.

A cookbook is a volume filled with STIRRING passages.

A chef claims that his plan to wrap all potatoes in aluminum covering has been FOILED!

What did the leopard say after eating a hearty meal?
   "Mmmm—that just hit the spot."

Who invented spaghetti?
  Someone who used his noodle.

"Excuse me," said Basil to Rosemary, "do you have the THYME?"

A lobster never comes ashore without great risk of getting into hot water.

"Do you serve crabs?" asked the old man.
"We serve anybody," answered the waiter.

What did the big skillet say to the little skillet?
  "Hello small fry."

Did you hear about the two fruit growers who got married?
  They made a perfect pear (pair).

How do you make an apple go bananas?
  You drive it out of its rind.

Customer: This coffee tastes like mud.
Waiter: That's because it was fresh ground this morning.

One man became the manager of a large doughnut bakery.
  He was in charge of the HOLE works.

One baker wanted to make certain that he'd rise early in the morning, so he ate some yeast at night!

There's one cook who signs his letters, LOVE AND QUICHES.

Why are cooks considered to be cruel?
  Because they beat the eggs and whip he cream.

Why do bakers work so hard?
  They knead the dough.

Why did the cookie cry?
  Because its mother had been a wafer so long.

Baby ear of corn: Mama, where did I come from?
Mama ear of corn: Hush dear—the *stalk* brought you

What do you call a husk of corn that is crying?
  Corn-on-the-sob.

Ivan didn't bother to go into the restaurant because he thought it was closed. The sign on the window read: HOME COOKING.

"Do you know the joke about the Cornflakes and the Rice Krispies who had a fight?"
  "No."
  "I can only tell you a little—it's a cereal (serial)."

"Mom made a terrible mistake at breakfast—she gave Dad soap-flakes instead of cornflakes."
  "Did he get angry?"
  "I'll say—he was foaming at the mouth!"

Husband: Are you sure this ham is cured?
Wife: That's what the butcher told me.
Husband: Well, if you ask me, I'd say it had a relapse!

Farmer Jones gave his neighbor a butter churn as a Christmas present, and his neighbor gave him one in return saying, "One good churn deserves another."

Did you hear about the waiter who was fired from his job because he was too independent? Apparently, he refused to take orders from anybody!

The impatient customer told the waiter, "Bring me some turtle soup—and make it *snappy!*"

A sign in a German cafeteria read:
MOTHERS, PLEASE WASH YOUR HANS
BEFORE EATING.

What's another name for a buffet car?
A chew-chew train.

The price of meat has got my mom in a perpetual stew.

Lamb is sheep at any price, but venison is always deer.

A new outdoor restaurant has just been opened.
It's called The Garden of Eatin'.

Waiter—a man who believes that money grows on trays.

Feast: an EAT-wave.

Waiter: Would you like some more alphabet soup?
Customer: No thank you. I couldn't manage another word.

Dairymaid—a girl who ought to know butter.

An Italian chef can best be judged by his *pasta* performance.

In feeding modern cowboys, today's chef has to be quick on the thaw!

My mom prepared shellfish for lunch. Daddy thought it was *shrimply* awful!

"Shall we have a salad?"
 "Yes—lettuce!"

My father wanted to open a horsemeat restaurant, but he couldn't *stirrup* any interest.

When the journalist asked the chef to tell him the ingredients he used in his delicious recipes, the chef replied "I'm sorry, I never reveal my sauces (sources)."

The cost of food is rising all the time. You might say it's becoming *gastronomical*!

The manager of a fish shop is opening late. But I suppose it's *batter* late than never.

What happened when fire broke out at the salami-processing plant?
    You never sausage a mess!

When the price of sugar rose considerably, some people began to raise Cain.

One woman ate ten platefuls of oysters. Everyone who watched thought she was very shellfish (selfish).

What did one raspberry say to the other?
  "We're in a real jam."

What did the jar of mayonnaise say when a man took off the lid?
  "Do you mind—I'm dressing!"

What did one dried grape say to the other?
  "There isn't any raisin why we can't escape."

Eat oysters if you want MUSSEL tone.

A very large order of Chinese food was delivered to the House of Representatives last week. It was said to weigh *won ton*.

"How do you like the peanuts?"
"They're not all they're cracked up to be."

A husband told his wife, "This chicken broth is really SOUPER!"

What did the lighthouse-keeper eat for breakfast every morning?
Beacon and eggs.

When was the first cooking oil bottled?
   On a FRYday.

Who do chefs correspond with?
   Their pan pals.

Did you hear about the restaurant that opened below a karate school? It only served chops.

News flash: Two tons of human hair which was to be made into wigs was stolen from a factory. The police are *combing* the area for clues.

What did the bald man say when his wife gave him a comb as a present for Christmas?
   "Thank you, darling—I'll never part with it."

Did you hear about the male lion who put extra hair around his neck and started living under an assumed mane?

First sheep: We're about to have all our wool shaved off.
Second sheep: Why, the mere idea of it is *shear* nonsense!

Samson loved Delilah until she *bald* him out.

A man who wears a wig has a head that is HAIR-conditioned.

What did the bald rabbit think of wearing?
   A HAREpiece.

Wife: My split hairs are becoming a real problem.
Bald husband: I don't have that problem—my hair split years ago.

A man who buys an expensive toupee on credit is in debt over his ears.

Why did the old man save his toupee?
   He thought of it as a family HAIRloom.

Don't worry about going bald. Remember the old saying—
HAIR TODAY, GONE TOMORROW.

Many people are overweight. They claim they want to be slim, but it's just wishful shrinking.

Putting on weight is the penalty for exceeding the feed limit.

An afternoon snack is known as the pause that refleshes.

Diet—the triumph of mind over platter.

Christmas is a time of year when people get a little SANTAmental.

Some adults think a Christmas stocking is just a childish hang-up.

If you go shopping during the busy Christmas season, you'll soon discover that most shoppers you meet are people who believe in brotherly SHOVE!

What most children would like for Christmas is something to separate the men from the toys!

What do monsters sing at Christmas?
    "Deck the halls with poison ivy, fa la la la la . . . "

What do gorillas sing at Christmas?
  "Jungle bells, jungle bells . . . "

At Christmas the werewolf said to his victims, "Best VICIOUS for the season!"

This might be hard to believe but mice send each other ChristMOUSE cards!

When holly is used for decoration, everyone has a BERRY Christmas.

When Santa Claus stops delivering presents for a few minutes to have a rest, it's known as a SantaPAUSE.

Santa Claus was spotted in the sky one night, and all the children started to clap. This is known as SantAPPLAUSE.

Not long ago Santa developed a fear of closed places and refused to go down any more chimneys. His illness was diagnosed as SANTA CLAUS-trophobia.

What did Santa reply when asked if he liked climbing down chimneys?
 "Soots me."

My father is so mean that when December comes he starts dreaming of a TIGHT Christmas.

One kid received a wool shirt for Christmas—he was *tickled* pink!

Who married Santa Claus?
   Mary Christmas.

Why is a turkey never hungry at Christmas?
   Because he always gets stuffed!

The governor asked the prisoners, "What kind of Christmas party do you think we should have this year?"
   The prisoners were all agreed, "An OPEN house."

What did the duck say when it finished its Christmas shopping?

"Just put it on my bill!"

Mrs. Claus: Hurry up, or you'll be late delivering presents to all the children.

Santa Claus: But its starting to rain, dear.

What did the beaver say to the Christmas tree?

So long—it's been nice gnawing you.

As the holiday season approached, the lumberjack thought to himself, "Only ten more CHOPPING days till Christmas."

"I finally got my radio working," said the radio ham exSTATICally.

Why do gardeners always laugh at jokes?
  Because they have a sense of humus.

What's the secret of a gardener's success?
  Trowel and error.

Organic gardeners are people who TILL it like it is.

Wife: Was the topsoil you bought expensive?
Husband: No—it was DIRT cheap!

What is grass?
   Something that grows by inches and dies by feet.

Some people use cows for cutting their grass. They claim they make great lawn MOOers.

Amateur gardeners—people who are sometimes victims of vicious plots.

What book do gardeners read?
   The Weeder's Digest.

THEY'RE MORE THAN
FUNNY...

THEY'RE LAUGH-OUT-LOUD
HYSTERICAL!